here are 20 amazing facts about dinosaurs :

1-Dinosaurs may have ended up massive, but they all came from eggs.

2-It's believed that birds we see today have evolved from the most interesting dinosaurs.

3-It has recently been discovered that some dinosaurs even had feathers.

4-The dinosaur with the longest name was the Micropachycephalosaurus, which means tiny, thick headed lizard!

5-Most dinosaurs had very small brains and were about as clever as modern reptiles.

6-The word dinosaur comes from the Greek language and means 'terrible lizard'. They were called this because of their huge size, not because they were particularly terrible!

7-Dinosaurs were the biggest animals ever to have walked on earth.

8-No one is completely sure how dinosaurs became extinct, but most think that it was because of a massive asteroid (huge rock from space) crashing into the earth, or a gigantic volcanic eruption, or both. It's still a mystery today.

9- The heaviest and longest dinosaur ever discovered was the Argentinosaurus, which reached heights of up to 37 metres!

10-The first dinosaur to be named was the Megalosaurus in 1824.

11-A person who studies dinosaurs is called a palaeontologist.

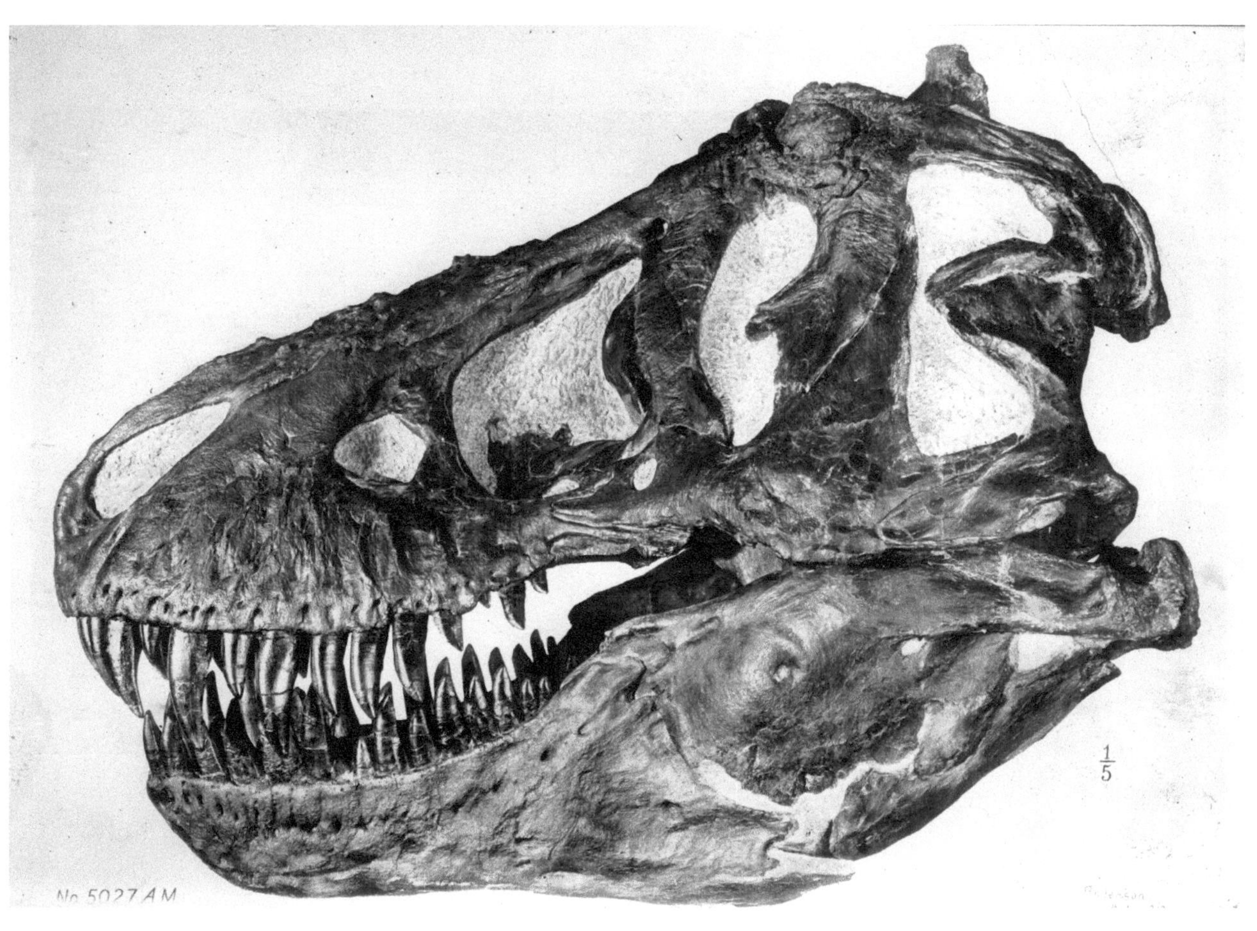

12-Although they're known for being massive monsters, many dinosaurs were actually smaller than a turkey.

13-The very biggest dinosaurs ate only plants. Those that ate meat were usually much smaller.

14-One reason that plant-eating dinosaurs grew so big was because they were so greedy. They could eat a huge amount of food very quickly. Sometimes, they swallowed up whole branches without chewing!

15-For their own protection, most plant-eating dinosaurs grew natural weapons like spikes and horns.

16-Dinosaurs lived on Earth for a far longer time than humans have, with their family trees stretching back many millions of years.

17-Unlike most animals alive these days, dinosaurs weren't warm OR cold blooded. They were somewhere in between.

18-Because dinosaurs were so different to anything alive today, no one is quite sure how long they lived for.

19-The largest meat-eating dinosaur that's been discovered was the Spinosaurus, which was around 50 foot long and spent most of its time in water.

20-Dinosaurs lived all across the world. Evidence of dinosaurs have been found on all seven of the world's continents through the discovery of dinosaur bones and fossils